THE
FACTS ON
ROMAN
CATHOLICISM

JOHN ANKERBERG
&JOHN WELDON

HARVEST HOUSE™ PUBLISHERS

EUGENE, OREGON

Unless otherwise indicated, Scripture verses are taken from the Holy Bible: New International Version® NIV®. Copyright © 1973, 1978, 1984 by the International Bible Society. Used by permission of Zondervan Publishing House. The "NIV" and "New International Version" trademarks are registered in the United States Patent and Trademark Office by International Bible Society.

Verses marked NASB are taken from the New American Standard Bible ®, © 1960, 1962, 1963, 1968, 1971, 1972, 1973, 1975, 1977 by The Lockman Foundation. Used by permission.

Cover by Terry Dugan Design, Minneapolis, Minnesota

THE FACTS ON ROMAN CATHOLICISM

Copyright © 1993 by The Ankerberg Theological Research Institute
Published by Harvest House Publishers
Eugene, Oregon 97402

Library of Congress Cataloging-in-Publication Data

Ankerberg, John, 1945-
    The facts on Roman Catholicism / John Ankerberg and John Weldon.
        p. cm. — (Facts on series)
    Originally published: Eugene, Or. : Harvest House, ©1993, in series:
    Ankerberg, John, 1945– Anker series.
    Includes bibliographical references.
        ISBN 0-7369-1110-3 (pbk.)
        1. Catholic Church—Controversial literature—Miscellanea. 2. Catholic
    Church—Doctrines—Miscellanea. I. Weldon, John. II. Title.
    BX1765.3 .A54 2003
    282—dc21   2002010767

All rights reserved. No part of this publication may be reproduced, stored in a retrieval system, or transmitted in any form or by any means—electronic, mechanical, digital, photocopy, recording, or any other—except for brief quotations in printed reviews, without the prior permission of the publisher.

Printed in the United States of America.

04 05 06 07 08 09 / VP-KB / 10 9 8 7 6 5 4 3 2

Contents

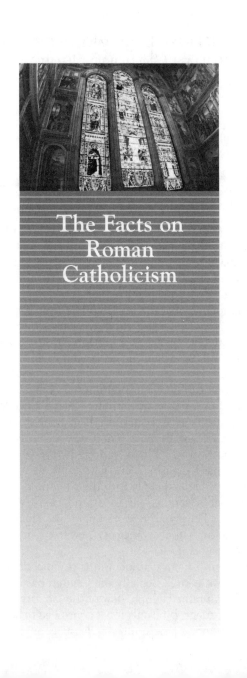

The Facts on
Roman
Catholicism

A BIBLICAL EVALUATION OF THE ROMAN CATHOLIC CHURCH

> The Catholic Church is the one true Church established by Jesus Christ for the salvation of all mankind (Rev. John A. O'Brien, *The Faith of Millions*, 46).

> You must teach what is in accord with sound doctrine (the apostle Paul's instructions to Titus, Titus 2:1).

The purpose of this book is twofold: 1) to help non-Catholic Christians better understand what Roman Catholicism believes and practices and 2) to help Roman Catholics evaluate their own church on the basis of biblical teaching. This is necessary since, as Catholic apologist Karl Keating correctly points out in *What Catholics Really Believe—Setting the Record Straight* (1992, p. 112), "Catholics are required to hold and believe all the declared doctrines of the Church."

No one can deny that substantial changes have occurred in the Roman Catholic Church since Vatican II, the major Roman Catholic council intended to usher in "the beginning of a new era in Roman Catholic history."[1] Since Vatican II, the Catholic Church has increasingly encouraged its members to read the Bible and apply it to their lives. Also, it is no longer a serious sin to attend non-Catholic churches. Perhaps the most important change in Catholicism is its allowance of a new freedom for the biblical gospel itself.

Modern Roman Catholicism is commendable in other ways as well. Socially the Church has consistently maintained a high view of the sanctity of life and of marriage. Biblically it has continued to defend the inerrancy of Scripture, at least as an official doctrine of the Church. Theologically it accepts the orthodox view of the Trinity, Christ's deity, and His atonement. Spiritually it has a good understanding of the seriousness of sin and its consequences in eternal judgment.

Nonetheless, all this does not mean that the Church is without problems. Perhaps the most serious issue in Roman Catholicism is its unwillingness to accept biblical authority alone as the final determiner of Christian doctrine and practice. For example, by accepting Catholic Tradition as a means of divine revelation, even biblically correct teachings in the Church become hedged about with unbiblical trimmings, which in turn tend to either revise, neutralize, or nullify the truth found in the Bible.

We agree with Dr. D. Martyn Lloyd-Jones (1899-1981) that, in many ways, the problem "is not so much a matter of 'denial' of the truth, but rather such an addition to the truth that eventually it becomes a departure from it."[2] This truly unfortunate situation illustrates a principle Jesus taught—that even heartfelt religious traditions can become a means of leading people away from God's best for their lives. On one occasion Jesus told the leading religious figures of His day, "You have let go of the commands of God and are holding on to the traditions of men" (Mark 7:8).

Regardless, no one can argue with the statement that "...the Roman Church has been one of the most powerful influences in the history of all civilization...."[3] Thus, because Roman Catholicism is a major world religion having more than a billion adherents,* and because its influence in the world is sizeable, a biblical evaluation of the teachings of the Church is vital.

---

* *The World Almanac 2002*, quoting *2001 Encyclopedia Britannica Book of the Year*.

1

Why should the issue of what constitutes divine revelation be a vital concern to all Christians?

If God has revealed Himself to mankind, can we know where that revelation is found? Can we identify it? In other words, can we truly know what God has spoken to us?

What constitutes divine revelation is crucial because without it, very little can be known about God—who He is, what He has communicated to us, and what He expects of us. The question of divine authority is inseparably bound to the issue of divine revelation. Only that which comes from God has divine authority. Only God's revelation has authentic and inherent power to command obedience.

Has God spoken? If so, where has He spoken?

Protestants have traditionally maintained that God has spoken solely in the 39 books of the Old Testament and the 27 books of the New Testament. Only these books are divinely authoritative.

In contrast, Roman Catholicism teaches that in addition to the Protestant Bible, there are five other sources having divine authority. First, there are additional books written between the Old and New Testaments, known to Catholics as the deutero-canonical books and to Protestants by the term "apocrypha." Roman Catholics consider these books genuine Scripture and include them as part of their Bible.[4] Second, Catholicism maintains that divine authority is to be found in the authorized Tradition of the Roman Catholic Church, which is also classified as the "Word of God."[5] Third, divine authority (infallibility) is given to the Pope when he speaks officially on matters of faith and morals.[6] Fourth, when speaking or teaching in conjunction with the Pope and orthodox Catholic Tradition, Roman Catholic bishops are also held to be infallible, and hence, divinely authoritative.[7] Finally, official Roman Catholic interpretation of the Bible (Catholic teaching) is considered to have divine warrant and authority.[8] In essence, all five of these sources can be summarized by the term "Roman Catholic Tradition."

Protestantism rejects these additional sources of divine authority, and this underscores the single most important division between the two churches. Neither Protestants nor Catholics can deny this issue. Divine authority cannot be found in the Bible alone and at the same time in various additional sources of alleged revelation *if* these deny the Bible. Because God does not contradict Himself (2 Corinthians 1:17-20; cf. Psalm 145:13; Galatians 3:21; Hebrews 13:8) and cannot lie (Titus 1:2), He cannot affirm one set of teachings in the Bible and then declare them wrong through additional forms of revealed Tradition. Therefore, Protestants believe that if the Bible truly is God's Word (as Catholics also maintain), then anything that conflicts with biblical teaching cannot possibly be from God.

In short, this issue is crucial because Catholic Tradition and biblical revelation conflict with one another on matters of vital importance, such as the means of salvation. In the end, this may have great personal consequence, including the uncertainty about or even the unintended rejection of the true means of salvation.

No one can deny that devout Catholics, like Protestants, sincerely wish to do God's will; they desire to know what is pleasing to God so they may live their lives accordingly. This is why the issue of biblical authority is so crucial.

2

Why do Protestants believe the Bible alone is authoritative and inerrant (free from error)?

As we will see, the Bible asserts or assumes its inerrancy throughout its pages. But it is important to realize that inerrancy is inseparably bound to both the doctrine of revelation as well as to the nature of God Himself. Why?

First, because God's revelation of Himself occurred through a very specific manner—"verbal, plenary inspiration." This means that the divine inspiration of the Bible involves its very words (Matthew 4:4; Romans 3:2) and extends to every part of Scripture. This is why the Bible claims "*All* Scripture is inspired by God..." (2 Timothy 3:16, NASB).

Second, the Bible reveals that God's nature is holy; therefore, He is incapable of lying. If divine inspiration extends to every word of the Bible, the entire Bible must be considered free of error. In other words, if God is incapable of inspiring error, whatever is inspired is inerrant.

Finally, the Bible also reveals that God is omnipotent or all powerful. This means He was able to safeguard the process of inspiration from error even though it was given through fallible men. In light of all this, it must be concluded that whatever God speaks is inerrant, and since every word of the Bible is God's word, therefore the Bible is without error.

Thus, in order to establish the Bible alone as the only source of divine authority, we need to prove that a) the Bible claims to be the inerrant Word of God, b) these claims are justified, and c) anything which contradicts what the Bible teaches cannot, logically, have divine authority.

A. Does the Bible claim to be the inerrant Word of God?

1. The Old Testament

The Old Testament is either God's Word or a fraud because it repeatedly asserts its divine authority (e.g., Isaiah 40:8). The term "thus says the Lord" or similar expressions are used some 2,800 times (Jeremiah 1:2; cf. Exodus 34:27; Deuteronomy 18:18; 1 Kings 22:14; Isaiah 8:19-20; Jeremiah 36:29; Amos 3). Inspiration (i.e., inerrancy) is explicitly asserted for almost 70 percent of the Old Testament, or 26 of 39 books.[9]

Further, New Testament assertions to the verbal, plenary inspiration of the Old Testament provide additional corroboration. Here we find that more than 90 percent of the Old Testament books "have their authority and/or authenticity directly affirmed by the New Testament."[10] For example, in the book of Hebrews the phrase "God said" or its equivalent occurs many times just prior to quoting specific books of the Old Testament such as Psalms (Hebrews 1:6-12; 4:7), Jeremiah (8:8-12; 10:15-17), Haggai (12:26), Deuteronomy (13:5), and others. Particularly relevant are the pronouncements of Jesus, who, as God incarnate, speaks infallibly (Matthew 24:35; John 5:46; 7:16; 8:14-16,26,28; 12:48-50; 14:6; cf. Philippians 2:1-8; Titus 2:13; 2 Peter 1:20-21; John 1:14). In John 17:17, Jesus said, "Thy Word is Truth" (NASB), and in Matthew 4:4, "Man shall not live by bread alone, but by every word that proceeds from the mouth of God" (NASB). In both instances He could only have referred to the Jewish Scriptures—our Protestant Old Testament (cf. Luke 24:27). Jesus affirms 100 percent of the Old Testament as inspired and inerrant.[11]

2. The New Testament

Jesus indicated more than once that new revelation from God was forthcoming. For example, He promised the disciples that the Holy Spirit would teach them all things and bring to remembrance the things they were taught (John 14:26), referring to the Gospels (cf. Matthew 24:35). He also promised that the Holy Spirit would guide them into all the truth (John 16:12-15), referring to the remainder of the New Testament. Thus, it is not surprising that:

> Virtually every New Testament writer claimed that his writing was divinely authoritative…. The cumulative effect of this self-testimony is an overwhelming confirmation that the New Testament writers claimed inspiration.[12]

Indeed, the fact that the New Testament writers assumed their writing was as binding as the Old Testament asserts a great deal. Such writers were orthodox Jews who believed God's Word was heretofore confined to the known Old Testament canon. To add to this body of holy writings was a terrible presumption unless inspiration were clearly present. But their recognition of inspiration is not so surprising. The very fact of the arrival of the long-prophesied *messiah* and the *new covenant* (as mentioned in Isaiah, Jeremiah, Ezekiel, etc.) coupled with the incarnation and atonement of God Himself (John 1:14; Philippians 2:1-9) *demanded* a corresponding body of divine literature to explain and expound these events. [This was also true for the activity of God in the old covenant (e.g., Galatians 3:8; cf. John 16:12-15).] God had no more likely candidates for this revelation than the apostles of His own Son, or those they approved. And for perhaps even more credibility, the former skeptic and persecuter of the church, the great apostle Paul, was commissioned by God to write a full fourth of the entire new revelation.

Is it credible to believe Jesus thought the Holy Spirit, the "Spirit of Truth," who inspired the New Testament (cf. John 16:13-15) would corrupt His own words or inspire error?

How could the incarnate God teach the infallibility of the divinely inspired Old Testament and not know the same condition would apply to the divinely inspired New Testament? Perhaps one reason Jesus never wrote anything was because He knew it was unnecessary: The Holy Spirit would inspire an inerrant Word. How else could He teach (or could we reasonably believe), "My words will never pass away" (Matthew 24:35)?

Regardless, is it proper to call *errant* writings "holy"? How is inspiration *divine* if it allows for the presence of truth *and* error? Is it not simply human and, like every other book, to be treated like every other book? If we answer "no" by appealing to its unique theological content, how do we really know such content is true?

If God's Word is eternal, how can it be flawed? What did God mean when He called His Word "holy," "perfect," "true," "righteous," "good," "trustworthy," and "pure"?

On this issue of inerrancy, the great expositor Charles Spurgeon once stated, "This is the book untainted by any error, but is pure, unalloyed, perfect truth. Why? Because God wrote it. Ah! charge God with error if you please; tell *Him* that His book is not what it ought to be…."[13]

B. How do we know the claims to the inspiration of the Bible are justified?

There are many converging lines of evidence that strongly indicate the Bible really is God's *only* revelation to mankind. For example, scores of detailed predictions of the future, which were later fulfilled, are found only in the Bible and can only be explained on the basis of divine inspiration.[14] But the area we wish to stress is simply the authority of Jesus Christ Himself. Did He ever express any doubts about Scripture? Did He warn His church that the New Testament canon would be incomplete or corrupted? It is a historical fact that Jesus is the only person in history who conquered death by raising Himself from the dead to live forever. He is the only person who makes it possible, through His sinless sacrifice, for His followers to enter God's Kingdom.[15] This proves the truth of His claims to be God incarnate. If so, then

He is an infallible authority, and in that role He declared the Old Testament the inspired Word of God, pre-authenticated the New Testament (Matthew 24:35; John 14:26), and personally inspired its final book (Revelation 1:1-3).

Indeed, the strength of the case for inerrancy can only be seen by a detailed study of Jesus' absolute trust in and use of Scripture.[16] For Jesus, what Scripture said, God said. Not once did He say, "This Scripture is in error" and proceed to correct it. If Jesus *was* God, then He was correct in His view of Scripture: The Bible truly is the inerrant, revealed Word of God.

If God cannot lie, never changes, and can be trusted to never contradict Himself, then only one conclusion follows: Whatever or whoever denies what God has revealed in the Bible cannot be from God. Nowhere in the Bible does God tell us to accept anything that contradicts what He has said is true in His Word. All this is why Protestants logically maintain that our spiritual allegiance is to God and to His Word alone. To give our allegiance to church traditions or people who claim divine authority but never establish it is to take away the rightful place God should occupy in our lives.

3

What are the different categories of modern Roman Catholicism?

There are approximately nine categories of Roman Catholic people around the world. The distinctions between them are not often clear because they can overlap or merge or blur into one another. Nor would individual Catholics necessarily appreciate or agree with such labels. But they will serve as convenient definitions for purposes of discussion.

1. *Nominal or Social Catholicism:* the Roman Catholicism of the largely uncommitted—perhaps those born or married into the Church but who have

little knowledge of Catholic theology and who are, in practice, Catholics in name only.

2. *Syncretistic/eclectic Catholicism:* the Roman Catholicism that is, to varying degrees, combined with and/or absorbed by the pagan religion of the indigenous culture in which it exists (e.g., as in Mexico and South America).

3. *Traditional or orthodox Catholicism:* the powerful conservative branch of Roman Catholicism that holds to historic church doctrines such as those reasserted at the Council of Trent in the sixteenth century.

4. *"Moderate" Catholicism:* the Roman Catholicism of Vatican II, which is neither entirely traditional nor entirely liberal.

5. *Modernist, liberal Catholicism:* the post-Vatican II "progressive" Roman Catholicism that, to varying degrees, rejects traditional doctrine.

6. *Ethnic or cultural Catholicism:* the Roman Catholicism often retained by migrants to America who use "their religion to provide a sense of belonging. They feel that not to be Roman Catholic is not to belong and to lose [their] nationality and roots."[17]

7. *Lapsed or apostate Catholicism:* the Roman Catholicism which involves alienated, backslidden, or apostate Catholics who are largely indifferent to the Catholic Church.

8. *Charismatic Catholicism:* the Roman Catholicism that seeks the "baptism of the Holy Spirit" and speaking in tongues and other spiritual gifts as signs of a deeper Catholic spirituality.

9. *Evangelical Catholicism:* the branch of former Roman Catholics who are truly evangelical and have rejected the unbiblical teachings of Rome, often deciding to remain in the Church to evangelize other Catholics.

The traditionalists are arguably the most influential segment of the Church because through the Pope, bishops, and orthodox priests, they occupy the center of power in Catholicism. Traditionalists believe that by being obedient to the Church, they are being obedient to God and Christ. They have been taught that whatever the Church decrees as orthodox belief and practice through its tradition is, by definition, the will of God.[18]

4

Have the basic doctrines of the Roman Catholic Church changed today?

With such a variety of modern Catholic expression, many people might assume that the doctrines of Rome itself have changed since Vatican II (1962–1965). While it is true the Church has undergone significant alterations, major, permanent doctrinal change is not one of them. This is conceded by both knowledgeable Catholics and non-Catholics. For example, Catholic apologist Karl Keating confesses, "The Catholic Church did not change any of its doctrines at Trent and it did not change any at Vatican II" and "…there has been no alteration at all in basic doctrines….The Catholic Church is still the sole true Church…."[19] An Evangelical Council on Catholicism likewise concluded, "…there are many indications that Rome is fundamentally the same as it has always been."[20] In 1964 no less an authority than Pope Paul VI affirmed that "nothing really changes in the traditional doctrine."[21] Another commentator noted, "Roman Catholicism does not change. At heart, it is the same as it ever was."[22]

Nevertheless, Rome is still not entirely what it used to be. Vatican II did institute many nondoctrinal (e.g., ecclesiastical) changes as well as significant alterations in the interpretation of traditional doctrine. These new interpretations have such elasticity that they have the practical effect of permitting fundamental doctrinal change for those who wish it. As Protestant theologian Millard J. Erickson observes in his *Christian Theology,*

> [Examining Catholic theology] is difficult because, whereas at one time there was a uniform, official position within Roman Catholicism on most issues, now there appears to be only great diversity. Official doctrinal standards still remain, but they are now supplemented, and in some cases, are seemingly contradicted, by later statements. Among these later statements are the conclusions of the Second Vatican Council and the published opinions of individual Catholic scholars.[23]

However, in spite of changes made at Vatican II (1962–1965), it is clear that the historic doctrines of Rome, which are handed down from its centralized teaching authority, basically remain the same. One area of concern to Protestants is the doctrine of salvation. We will introduce this subject with a discussion of the Catholic sacraments.

5

What are the sacraments, and how do they function in the life of a Catholic believer?

The sacraments of Catholicism involve spiritual activities such as baptism, confirmation, penance, and participation in the Mass. These are presided over by a Catholic priest who acts as a mediator between God and man. These special activities are held to dispense God's "grace" (here, as a spiritual substance or power) and God's favor.

Rome's sevenfold sacramental system was apparently initiated for the first time in the twelfth century and continues today: "For the Roman Catholic his whole life from the cradle to the grave, and indeed beyond the grave in purgatory, is conditioned by the sacramental approach."[24] Thus, understanding the sacraments is essential to understanding Catholicism.

Through the sacraments, "…internal grace is that [power] received in the interior of the soul, enabling us to act supernaturally."[25] Further, "the supernatural gift of God infused into the very essence of the soul as a habit is habitual grace. This grace is also called *sanctifying* or *justifying* grace, because it is included in both…."[26]

The real difference between the Protestant and Catholic view of sacraments is not in the number of sacraments, two versus seven, but rather in the meaning and purpose of the sacraments. Protestantism sees its sacraments—baptism and communion—primarily as symbols and memorials of vital theological truths. But Catholicism sees the sacraments as actually changing a person inwardly, as if through a form of spiritual empowering. In Protestantism a sacrament *underscores a promise* of God; in Catholicism the sacraments *infuse a special grace into the soul* in order to meet a special need. Catholic sacraments are an outward sign of an infused grace.

We have summarized the results of each of the sacraments below:

- *Baptism* (which is not repeated) cleanses from original sin, removes other sins and consequent punishments, provides spiritual rebirth or regeneration (John 3:3), begins the process of justification, and is "necessary for salvation."[27]

- *Confirmation* (not repeated) bestows the Holy Spirit in a special sense, leading to "an increasing of sanctifying grace and the gifts of the Holy Spirit" as well as other spiritual power and a sealing to the Catholic Church.[28]

- *Penance* removes the penalty of sins committed after baptism and confirmation. Mortal or "deadly" sins are remitted and the "justification" lost by such sins is restored as a continuing process.[29]

- *Holy Eucharist* is where Christ is *resacrificed* and the benefits of Calvary are continually applied anew to the believer.[30]

- *Marriage* is where grace is given to remain in the bonds of matrimony in dictates with the requirements of the Catholic Church.[31]

- *Anointing the sick* (formerly *extreme unction*) bestows grace on those who are sick, old, or near death and helps in forgiveness of sins and sometimes the physical healing of the body.[32]

- *Holy orders* (not repeated) confers special grace and spiritual power upon bishops, priests, and deacons for leadership in the Church as representatives of Christ "for all eternity."[33]

The Catholic Council of Trent (1545–63), whose decrees remain authoritative, declared as "anathema" (divinely cursed) anyone who would deny the seven sacraments of Rome: "If anyone says that the sacraments…were not all instituted by our Lord Jesus Christ, or that there are more or less than seven…or that any one of these seven is not truly and intrinsically a sacrament, let him be anathema."[34] Further, "if anyone says that the sacraments…are not necessary for salvation…and that without them…men obtain from God through faith alone the grace of justification…let him be anathema."[35] Canon Five reads, "If anyone says that baptism is optional, that is, not necessary for salvation, let him be anathema."[36]

What this means is that Catholicism offers what is termed a *sacerdotal* salvation—a salvation that is given through the functions of the priesthood, namely the sacraments. In the end, salvation is a function of 1) God's grace, 2) individual faith and works, and 3) the Roman Catholic system of sacraments. (This is why the Church has *traditionally* taught that there is only one true Church—Rome—and that those outside of the Church cannot be saved since they are partakers of neither the one true Church nor the sacraments, both of which help procure salvation.) In our next two questions we will

20

see what the Bible teaches about salvation and then compare this with the Catholic view of salvation in greater detail.

6
What does the Bible teach concerning salvation?

The Bible teaches that salvation is something that comes freely to any individual who places genuine trust in Jesus Christ for forgiveness of sins. Thus, the Bible teaches that salvation is by grace through faith *alone*, entirely apart from personal merit or works of righteousness. Please read the following verses:

> For God so loved the world that he gave his one and only son, that whoever *believes* in him shall *not* perish but *have* eternal life (John 3:16, emphasis added).

> All the prophets testify about him [Jesus] that everyone who *believes* in him *receives forgiveness of sins* through his name (Acts 10:43, emphasis added).

> In him we *have* redemption through his blood, the *forgiveness of sins*, in accordance with the riches of God's grace…(Ephesians 1:7, emphasis added).

> For it is *by grace you have been saved*, through faith—and this *not* from yourselves, it is the *gift* of God—*not by works*, so that *no one* can boast (Ephesians 2:8-9, emphasis added).

> [Jesus was] sacrificed for [our] sins *once for all* when he offered himself (Hebrews 7:27, emphasis added).

> Therefore he is able to *save completely* those who come to God through him, because he always lives to intercede for them (Hebrews 7:25, emphasis added).

> …But he [Jesus] entered the Most Holy Place once for all by his own blood, *having obtained* eternal redemption.…[He] offered *for all time* one sacrifice for sins…because by *one sacrifice* he has *made perfect forever* those who *are being* made holy. The Holy Spirit also testifies to us about this…he says: "…Their sins

and lawless acts *I will remember no more*" (Hebrews 9:12; 10:12,14-15,17, emphasis added).

Do any of these verses teach that salvation—or forgiveness of sins—comes by good works, through religious sacraments, or by any other means of human merit? Do these Scriptures even hint that salvation comes by being good or by personal effort? No. God's Word teaches that complete salvation occurs solely by faith in what Christ already accomplished on the cross 2,000 years ago.

Because salvation is by grace through faith *alone*, this means that once a person has trusted in Christ, then he may *know* that his sins are forgiven—*all sins*—past, present, and future. "He forgave us *all* our sins…" (Colossians 2:13, emphasis added). (When Christ paid the full divine penalty for our sins 2,000 years ago, *all* our sins were future. If the Bible teaches our sins are forgiven at the point of true faith in Christ, this must include all of them, even future sins.) Therefore, come what may in life (see Romans 8:28-39), the person who trusts in Christ alone for salvation *will* go to heaven when he dies because God informs that person he now possesses "an inheritance that can *never* perish, spoil or fade" because it is "*kept* in heaven for you…" (1 Peter 1:4-5, emphasis added).

The salvation God offers is perfectly secure pre-cisely *because* it involves a gracious act of God and is in no way dependent upon human merit or works for its accomplishment:

> I tell you the truth, whoever hears my word and believes him who sent me *has eternal life* and will *not* be condemned; he *has crossed over* from death to life (John 5:24, emphasis added).

> I tell you *the truth*, he who believes *has* everlasting life (John 6:47, emphasis added).

> I write these things to you who *believe* in the name of the Son of God so that you may *know* that you *have eternal life* (1 John 5:13, emphasis added).

22

Again, these verses teach that people can *know* they *now* possess eternal life merely by their personal trust in Jesus. If any person has *eternal* life, it cannot be lost, can it? Nor can it subsequently be earned, can it? However, the above Scriptures do not reflect the teaching of the Catholic Church, which maintains that salvation is a provisional, lifelong *process* partially earned by a person's own good works and individual merit.

Biblically, full salvation in the sense of forgiveness of all sins and a right standing before God occurs at a *point* in time—the point of receiving Christ as personal Savior—even though the practical implications of salvation (e.g., progressive *sanctification* or growth in holiness) are worked out over a lifetime. Thus, 1) complete *reconciliation* with God (full forgiveness of sins and cancellation of the penalty of sin), 2) *regeneration* (being made spiritually alive to God and the imparting of eternal life), and 3) *justification* (the crediting of Christ's full and complete righteousness to the believer) all occur in an *instant*, at the *moment* of saving faith. Further, they are irrevocable since they are all gifts from God, and God says that He never takes back what He gives (Romans 11:29).

Catholicism, on the other hand, teaches that a right standing before God is not something that can happen fully in this life, nor can it occur in a moment of time. Rather, it is something that comprises a very lengthy process that is earned only after a lifetime of good works and obtained merit and—in all likelihood—tremendous personal suffering in purgatory after death to cleanse the remnants of sin and judicially perfect the believer.

Here, the contrasts between the biblical view of salvation and the Roman Catholic view could not be clearer. The following material further illustrates the constrasts and will also prepare us for the next three questions.

Grace

Bible: A *disposition* of God toward mankind expressing His mercy and love so that the believer is now treated *as if* he were innocent and perfectly righteous.

Catholicism: A *substance* or *power* separate from God that is placed into a believer to enable him to perform meritorious works and earn the "right" to heaven.

Salvation

Bible: The instantaneous reception of an eternally irrevocable right standing before God, secured at the point of faith entirely by grace. Salvation is given to those whom the Bible describes as "ungodly," "sinners," "enemies," and "children of wrath" (e.g., Romans 5:6-10; Ephesians 2:1) and, thus, to those who are not objectively righteous.

Catholicism: The lifelong process whereby God and mankind cooperate in the securing of forgiveness of sin. This is achieved only after death (and/or purgatorial cleansing from sin) and is dependent on man's personal securing of *objective* righteousness before God; otherwise, there is no salvation.

Reconciliation (through atonement)

Bible: All sins are forgiven at the point of salvation—past, present, and future—because Christ's death satisfied all God's wrath against sin. (See Colossians 2:13.)

Catholicism: Sins are only potentially forgiven and so must be worked off through a process mediated by the Church and its sacraments over the lifetime of the believer.

Regeneration

Bible: The instantaneous imparting of eternal life and the quickening of the human spirit, making it alive to God.

Catholicism: In part, the lifelong process of infusing grace (spiritual power) to perform works of merit.

Justification

Bible: The legal declaration of Christ's righteousness reckoned to the believer at the point of faith solely as an act of God's mercy.

Catholicism: Spiritual rebirth and the lifelong process of sanctification, which begins at the point of the sacrament of baptism.

7

What does the Catholic Church teach concerning salvation?

Catholic popes have historically emphasized the belief that, in the words of John Paul II, "Man is justified by works and not by faith alone."[37]

Despite changes in Catholicism, most priests remain loyal to Rome. Perhaps this explains why, according to one of the most thorough polls of American clergy ever made, "over three-quarters of Roman Catholic priests *reject* the view that our only hope for heaven is through personal faith in Jesus Christ as Lord and Savior. They hold instead that 'heaven is a divine reward for those who earn it by their good life.'" Priestly loyalty to Rome may also explain why this poll revealed that "four-fifths of all priests *reject* the Bible as the first place to turn in deciding religious questions; rather, they test their religious beliefs by what the Church says."[38]

The majority of Catholic priests deny the biblical doctrine of salvation because *as priests*—loyal to the Pope—they are required to reject the idea that divine authority resides only in the Bible. For them, divine authority resides in the Catholic Church *and* Tradition. Priests, therefore, look primarily to the Church for answers to religious questions because they believe only the Catholic Church can infallibly determine proper doctrine through its interpretation of the Bible. Thus, a study of Catholic history will show that it is the *Church*, and not the *Bible*, that has developed Catholic doctrine over the years. These doctrines are, in part, upheld by the unique definition Rome gives to biblical words.

For example, Catholic writers often speak of "salvation by grace" or state emphatically that "good works can't earn salvation"—and they will cite biblical Scriptures to that effect. But they mean something different than what the Bible means. They are reiterating the position of the Council of Trent that no one can do good works or please God apart from the prior infusing of sanctifying grace. *But*—and this is key—Catholic theology goes on to teach that these very works which are inspired by grace *are*, in the end, what helps to save a person.

It is crucial to realize that once terms such as "faith," "grace," "salvation," "redemption," and "justification" are interpreted through larger Catholic theology, they become so altered that they *lose* their biblical meaning.*

Karl Keating is entirely correct when he points out, "As in so many matters, fundamentalists [e.g., conservative Christians] and Catholics are at loggerheads because they define terms differently."[40]

Devout Catholics do not question their Church's teaching about its definitions of biblical terms because the Catholic Church emphasizes that "over the Book [Bible] stands the Church...."[41] The Church has final authority over the Bible and, therefore, it is the Church's interpretation of biblical words that are authoritative. In the end, it is the Church's definition of biblical terms—and not the Bible's—that wins the day.

---

* For example, the words used in Canons 1 and 3 of the Council of Trent concerning justification sound completely biblical[39]—until they are interpreted in light of larger Catholic theology. Then they mean something entirely different than what the Bible means.

Thus, *The Papal Encyclicals* correctly state that while Protestants turn to the Bible to determine whether or not a doctrine is true,

> this is just the reverse of the Catholic's approach to belief. As the Catholic sees it, he must accept God on God's terms and not his own. It is not for him to "judge" the divine message, but only to receive it. Since he receives it from a living, teaching organ, he does not have to puzzle over the meaning of the revelation because the ever present living *magisterium* [teaching office] can tell him exactly what the doctrine intends.[42]

Again, Catholics turn to the Church because they have been promised that the Church exercises an *inerrant* authority to properly interpret the Bible. The Catholic believes he can, in full trust, accept whatever the Church teaches and never worry that the Church might be wrong.

In his definitive critique of the Council of Trent (a council convened to oppose Protestant teaching), eminent Lutheran theologian Martin Chemnitz (1522–1586) correctly noted that the Catholic popes and teaching office had reserved for themselves the prerogative of a biased interpretation of Scripture predicated primarily upon Catholic Tradition. The end result was an entirely new interpretation "so that we must believe not what the Scripture says simply, strictly, and clearly, but what they through their power and authority interpret for us. By this strategy they seek to escape the clearest passages [of Scripture] concerning justifying faith...the intercession of Christ, etc."[43]

In sharp contrast to the Bible, the Catholic doctrine of salvation teaches or implies that actual forgiveness of sins comes not only by faith in Christ, but also through many or all of the following: a) the sacraments, such as baptism and penance; b) participation in the Mass; c) the help of the virgin Mary; d) the recitation of the rosary; and e) purgatorial suffering after death. Because the true merit of man, achieved through these and other means, is in some sense responsible for salvation, Catholicism cannot logically deny that it teaches a form of salvation by works. A brief discussion of these five points will bear this out.

A. The Sacraments

In *Fundamentals of Catholic Dogma*, Dr. Ludwig Ott observed, "The Sacraments are the means appointed by God for attainment of eternal salvation. Three of them are in the ordinary way of salvation *so necessary* that without their use *salvation cannot be attained* [i.e., baptism, penance, holy orders]."[44]

1. Baptism. The Catholic Church teaches that baptism remits original sin, actual guilt, and all punishment due to sin.[45] The Catholic Church also teaches that baptism confers 1) justification, 2) spiritual rebirth or regeneration, and 3) sanctification. Catholic apologist Karl Keating says, "The Catholic Church has always taught that justification comes through the sacrament of baptism" and "baptism is the justifying act."[46] Thus, "the justification that occurs at baptism effects a real change in the soul..."[47]

The Catholic Encyclopedia further explains the importance of baptism in the scheme of salvation:

> The effects of this sacrament are: 1) it cleanses us from original sin; 2) it makes us Christians through grace by sharing in Christ's death and resurrection and setting up an initial program of living...; 3) it makes us children of God as the life of Christ is brought forth within us....Vatican II declared: "...baptism constitutes a sacramental bond of unity linking all who have been reborn by means of it. Baptism, of itself, is only a beginning. [But]...baptism is *necessary for salvation*...."[48]

Baptism, however, is only the *beginning* of justification because in Catholic teaching subsequent good works *increase* grace (spiritual power) and help perfect justification.

2. Penance. Penance is a particular act, or acts, considered as satisfaction offered to God as a reparation for sin committed.[49] Penance may involve mortification, such as wearing an irritating shirt woven of coarse animal hair,[50] prayer, a religious pilgrimage to a shrine of Christ or Mary,[51] or any number of other deeds.

According to *The Catholic Encyclopedia*, Jesus Christ instituted the sacrament of penance for "the pardon of sins committed after baptism."[52] Thus, "in the sacrament of penance, the faithful obtain from the mercy of God pardon for their sins against Him...."[53]

As noted, the sacrament of penance is designed specifically to deal with sins committed after baptism. Why? Because the grace that is received or infused in baptism can be entirely lost by mortal ("deadly") sin. Mortal sin is held to be deadly because it actually destroys the grace of God within a person, making salvation necessary again. Thus, a new sacrament (penance) is necessary in order to restore an individual to the state of grace first received at baptism.

In fact, without penance a person *cannot* be restored to salvation. Penance is related to the concept of justification in such a way that it actually "restores" the process of justification. In one sense, this is why the Council of Trent referred to the sacrament of penance as the "second plank" of justification.[54]

Through penance the Roman Catholic believer (in part, on a human level) actually makes atonement or satisfaction for his own sins. This would seem to say that, in a very real sense, the death of Christ alone was insufficient to cover the penalty of those sins completely.

3. *Priestly confession* (dictated by *Holy Orders*). Although it is frequently lost upon the faithful, the Catholic Church has made it clear that in personal confession of sin, the priest does *not* have intrinsic authority to forgive a person's sins. His only authority is a derived one in that he is a representative for Christ, and that Christ is working through him. Thus, when the priest says, "I absolve you," he does not mean that he alone is absolving a person from his or her sins; it is Christ through him. Nevertheless, priestly confession is said to be necessary for salvation.

Further, because Christ actually is, in Person, working through the priest (who may be called "another Christ"), his absolution is as valid as if done by Christ Himself.[55] In *Fundamentals of Catholic Dogma* we read, "Confession is the self-accusation by the penitent of his sins before a fully empowered priest, in order to obtain forgiveness from him by virtue of the power of the keys....The Sacramental confession of sins is ordained by God and *is necessary for salvation.*"[56]

B. The Mass

Although it claims that the Mass in no way detracts from the atonement of Christ, the Catholic Church nevertheless believes that it is principally through the Mass that the blessings of Christ's death are applied to believers. Catholics teach that in the Mass Christ is actually, in a real sense, resacrificed. It is not a *recrucifixion* of Christ (He does not literally suffer and die again), but it is much more than merely a memorial service. Karl Keating, director of "Catholic Answers," cites Rev. John A. O'Brien as correctly describing the Mass: "The Mass is the renewal *and perpetuation* of the sacrifice of the Cross in the sense that it offers anew to God the Victim of Calvary...and applies the fruits of Christ's death upon the cross to individual human souls."[57]

Because the fruit of Christ's death is actually *applied* at the Mass, one can see why Catholics attach such importance to this practice. *The Catholic Catechism* cites the Council of Trent as providing the standard Catholic view: "This sacrifice [of the Mass] *is truly propitiatory*...through the Mass we obtain mercy and find grace to help in time of need. For by this oblation the Lord is appeased...and *he pardons wrong doing and sins, even grave ones.*"[58]

Another standard Catholic work observes, "In the Sacrifice of the Mass, Christ's sacrifice on the cross is made present, its memory is celebrated, and its saving power is applied."[59] Thus, "as a propitiatory sacrifice…the Sacrifice of the Mass effects the remission of sins and the punishment for sins…."*[61]

C. The Role of Mary

Catholicism officially teaches that Mary's role in salvation in no way detracts from that of Christ. However, the Catholic Church also teaches that Mary played a vital part in the forgiveness of sins and in the salvation of the world. In *The Christ of Vatican II*, we are told that both the Scriptures and Tradition "show the role of the Mother of the Savior in the economy of salvation," that she freely cooperated *"in the work of human salvation* through faith and obedience," and that therefore, "The union of the Mother with the Son *in the work of salvation* is made manifest from the time of Christ's virginal conception up to His death."[62]

As *The Catholic Encyclopedia* observes, "Mary was not subject to the law of suffering and death, which are penalties of the sin of human nature, even though she knew these, experienced them, and endured them *for our salvation*."[63] (For more information on the role of Mary, see Question 13.)

D. The Rosary

According to Tradition, the Rosary supplies a Catholic with spiritual power, as well as many blessings and graces from God. Pope Paul VI affirmed in his Apostolic Exhortation *Marialis Cultus* (February 2, 1974) that the Rosary was the pious practice which is "the compendium of the entire gospel."[64] Thus, he emphasized that "the Rosary should be considered as one of the best and most efficacious prayers…that the Christian family is invited to recite."[65]

---

* The Sacrifice of the Mass does not remit the guilt of sins immediately as do the sacraments of baptism and penance, but mediately by the conferring of the grace of repentance. The Council of Trent teaches: "Propitiated by the offering of the sacrifice [Mass], God, by granting the grace and the gift of penance remits trespasses and sins, however grievous they may be."[60]

The Rosary is made up of both mental prayer and vocal prayer. In mental prayer the participant meditates on the major "mysteries" (particular events) of the life, death, and glories of Jesus and Mary. The vocal aspect involves the recitation of fifteen "decades" (portions) of the "Hail Mary" which involves contemplating fifteen principal virtues that were practiced by Jesus and Mary. One Catholic author writes, "...the Rosary recited with meditation on the mysteries brings about the following marvelous results: it gradually gives us a perfect knowledge of Jesus Christ; *it purifies our souls, washing away sin*; it gives us victory over all our enemies....It supplies us with what is needed to *pay all our debts to God* and to our fellow men, and finally, it obtains all kinds of graces for us from almighty God."[66]

E. Purgatory

Catholicism believes that penance may be performed by good works in this life or through hellish suffering endured in purgatory after death. Those in purgatory are labeled as "the Church Suffering...who have died in grace and whose souls are being purged in purgatory."[67] Thus, "the temporal punishments for sins are atoned for in the purifying fire [of purgatory]...by the willing bearing of the expiatory punishments imposed by God."[68]

Purgatorial suffering is justified on the following basis: Because no one can enter heaven with any stain of sin whatever, "anyone less than perfect must first be purified before he can be admitted to [heaven]."[69] Although technically the souls in purgatory cannot make true satisfaction for their sins,[70] the fact of being in purgatory and enduring punishment for them is believed to both cleanse individuals of the remnants of sin and permit such persons entrance into heaven as newly perfected people.[71]

In purgatory the person pays for the penalty of venial or mortal sin, even if the guilt of those sins has already been forgiven by the sacrament of penance.[72]

The Catholic Encyclopedia teaches,

> The souls of those who have died in the state of grace
> suffer for a time a *purging that prepares them* to enter
> heaven....The purpose of purgatory is *to cleanse one of
> imperfections, venial sins, and faults*, and to remit or do
> away with the temporal punishments due to mortal
> sins that have been forgiven in the Sacrament of
> Penance. It is an intermediate state in which the
> departed souls *can atone for unforgiven sins* before
> receiving their final reward....Such "purgatorial pun-
> ishments" may be relieved by the offerings of the living
> faithful, such as Masses, prayers, alms, and other acts
> of piety and devotion.[73]

We have now briefly examined what the
Catholic Church teaches concerning forgiveness of
sins and 1) the sacraments, such as baptism and
penance, 2) the Mass, 3) the Virgin Mary, 4) the
Rosary, and 5) purgatorial suffering. In some sense,
Catholicism teaches that *all* these practices remit
sin or the guilt of sin.

But the Bible teaches that *full* forgiveness of sin,
including its penalty, occurs solely by grace through
faith in Jesus Christ *alone*, based upon the complete
adequacy of His death on the cross, which was a *full*
propitiatory atonement. Catholic teaching, on the
other hand, *implies* (at least) the death of Christ was
in some sense insufficient in these areas. While
Catholics may disagree with this assessment, it seems
to be the logical conclusion of their own beliefs and
practices.

Karl Keating's book, *Catholicism and Fundamentalism*, offers the standard Catholic position on salvation. He opposes the biblical teaching of salvation
by grace through faith alone. He emphasizes that, in
Catholicism, men and women learn that they will
merit heaven by their good works and personal righteousness, but that to merely "accept Jesus" as Savior
accomplishes nothing:

> For Catholics, salvation depends on the state of the
> soul at death. Christ...did his part, and now we have
> to *cooperate* by doing ours. If we are to pass through

those [heavenly] gates, we have to be in the right spiritual state....The Church teaches that only souls that *are objectively good* and *objectively pleasing* to God *merit* heaven, and such souls are ones filled with sanctifying grace....As Catholics see it, anyone can *achieve* heaven, and anyone can *lose* it....The apparent saint can throw away salvation at the last moment and end up no better off than the man who *never did* a good deed in his life. It all depends on how one enters death, which is why dying is by far one's most important act....[What this means is that] "accepting Jesus" has nothing to do with turning a spiritually dead soul into a soul alive with sanctifying grace. The soul [that "accepts Jesus"] remains the same [i.e., dead]....The Reformer saw justification as a mere legal act by which God declares the sinner to be meriting heaven....The Catholic Church, not surprisingly, understands justification differently. It sees it as a true eradication of sin and a true sanctification and renewal. The soul becomes *objectively pleasing* to God and so *merits* heaven. It *merits* heaven because now it is *actually good*....The Bible is quite clear that we are saved by faith. The Reformers were quite right in saying this, and to this extent they merely repeated the constant teaching of the Church. Where they erred was in saying that we are saved by faith *alone*.*[74]

But if the Bible teaches that salvation is entirely by *grace*, then salvation *is* by faith alone. To add meritorious works would mean that salvation is by faith *and* works. And the Bible clearly indicates that the concepts of "grace salvation" and "works salvation" involve opposing principles. One cannot have a salvation based 75 percent on grace and 25 percent on works—it is entirely one or entirely the other. Thus, Scripture emphasizes, "And if [salvation is] by grace, then it is no longer by works; if it were, grace would no longer be grace" (Romans 11:6).

---

* In "My Ticket to Heaven," a popular Catholic tract, the reader is told that his "ticket to heaven" is good works and permanent abstention from mortal sin (pp. 3-10). Thus, "If I do my part, God will do His part" (p. 12). This booklet is labeled as "a tract of salvation," and a straightforward presentation of Christian faith, but its principal effect is to produce the fear of never achieving heaven since salvation is so clearly laid out as involving a practical perfectionism. Written by a priest, it never once mentions personal faith in Jesus Christ as the basis for salvation.

8

What does the Bible teach about the doctrine of justification?

This is perhaps the most important subject in this book because no doctrine is more crucial—nor more misunderstood and neglected, even by Protestants—than the biblical doctrine of justification by faith alone.

The Bible teaches that any person who truly believes in Jesus Christ as his or her personal Savior from sin is *at that point* irrevocably and eternally justified. What is justification? Justification is the act of God whereby He not only forgives the sins of believers, but He also declares them perfectly righteous by reckoning or imputing the obedience and righteousness of Christ Himself to them through faith. It might help to look at it this way: If a wealthy uncle deposits a million dollars to the checking account of his young nephew, that money is now the property of his nephew even though the lad never earned it, worked for it, or deserved it. In justification, God "deposits" the righteousness of Christ to the believer's account—He credits the Christian with the moral perfection of His own Son. Justification is a completed act of God, and because it is entirely accomplished by God, once for all, it is not a lifelong process as is personal sanctification (individual growth in holy living).

The following Scriptures clearly show that justification is 1) a *crediting* of righteousness on the basis of a person's faith alone; 2) a completed act of God; and 3) something that occurs wholly apart from personal merit or good works.

> ...to the man who...trusts God who justifies the wicked, *his faith is credited* as righteousness....[How blessed is] the man to whom God *credits righteousness* apart from works (Romans 4:5-6, emphasis added).

> For we maintain that a man is justified *by faith* apart from works of the Law (Romans 3:28, NASB, emphasis added). (See also Philippians 3:9.)

> Therefore *having been* justified by faith, we *have peace* with God through our Lord Jesus Christ (Romans 5:1, NASB, emphasis added).

> Much more then, having now *been justified by His blood,* we *shall be saved* from the wrath of God through Him (Romans 5:9, NASB, emphasis added; cf. Romans 9:30–10:4; 1 Corinthians 6:11; Galatians 2:16; 3:8-9,21,24).

Unfortunately, some Catholics have misunderstood the Protestant position here, thinking it means that mere assent to doctrine saves entirely and that Protestants have little concern for good works or sanctification. To the contrary, Scripture is clear that good works and sanctification are crucial—indeed it is the very knowledge of grace itself (in a Protestant sense) that produces good works and growth in holy living (see Ephesians 2:8-10; 1 Peter 5:12; 2 Peter 3:18; Colossians 1:6; cf. 2:23). But good works and sanctification have nothing to do with our justification. What justification means to Protestants is that believers are to plead the merits of *Christ* before the throne of God, instead of their *own* merits. This is why biblical Christians accept the "*gift* of righteousness" (Romans 5:17) and "glory in Christ Jesus and put no confidence in the flesh" (Philippians 3:3, NASB).

Justification means that a Christian may be assured that, in *God's* eyes, he now possesses the perfect holiness necessary to gain entrance to heaven. Why? If the death of Christ forgave *all* sins and *fully* satisfied the divine penalty due them, and if God *declares* believers absolutely righteous on the basis of their faith in Christ, then nothing else is *needed* to permit their entrance into heaven. Because of justification—i.e., because Christ's righteousness and merits are reckoned to the believer (as far as God is concerned)—the Christian now possesses perfect holiness *in this life,* and he possesses it *from the moment* of saving faith. He cannot attain it by himself, nor does he need sacraments, indulgences, the Rosary, or purgatory in order to enter heaven. This is what the biblical doctrine of justification means.[75]

9

What does the Roman Catholic Church teach about the doctrine of justification?

The Catholic Church has never denied that justification is by an act of God's grace. In fact, Catholic writers often sound perfectly biblical—and this is what leads to confusion. For example, consider the plain answer given to the question, "How is the sinner justified?" in Stephen Keenan's *Doctrinal Catechism:* "He is justified gratuitously by the pure mercy of God, not on account of his own or any human merit, but purely through the merits of Jesus Christ; for Jesus Christ is our only mediator of redemption, who alone, by his passion and death, has reconciled us to his Father."[76]

The problem here is *not* that Catholics teach that "justification occurs by grace." The problem is that the Catholic *definition* of "justification" and "grace" is different from what the Bible teaches. The Catholic Church teaches that justification is the *infusion* of sanctifying grace or supernatural ability which actually works to help make a person objectively righteous and pleasing in the eyes of God. If sustained until death, this grace permits one to *merit* entrance into heaven because of the righteous life he or she lived. One actually *deserves* heaven because one's own goodness, in part, has *earned* it. This explains why the basis for justification in Catholic theology is not the fact of Christ's righteousness being reckoned (imputed) to a believer by faith alone. Rather it is the fact that, through the sacraments, Christ's righteousness is infused into our very being so that we progressively become more and more righteous. And on that basis—the fact we have actual righteousness now—we are declared "righteous." Thus, in Catholicism justification occurs primarily by means of the sacraments and not exclusively by personal faith in Jesus Christ.

Now, the Church argues that because this infusion of sanctifying ability is not merited by anyone, it is therefore entirely a free gift of God's grace. But what this really seems to say is that God gives the means by which individuals can help to earn their own salvation. In the end, what saves us is the works we do after conversion that have been energized by grace. Let's explain this more fully.

In Catholic theology, infused grace is a spiritual power or strength given to believers that enables them to perform meritorious works. When believers cooperate with this grace and make good use of it, they gain the power to become just and righteous in themselves. If we have this "grace" (i.e., a power or substance) within us, we can then literally earn our way to heaven. How? By cooperating with the habitual grace within us, we can arrive at a state of actual righteousness. It is at *this* point only that we are then "declared" to be "just" because, in fact, we are objectively righteous. By further cooperating with God's grace and through individual performance of merit, we actually increase our grace and justification.[77] Because "the soul becomes good and holy through the infusion of grace"[78] as these are increased throughout life, a person naturally dies in a state of grace. Then he enters purgatory to pay the final penalty for his sins and to await his heavenly reward. In a very real sense, then, Catholic justification is simply God's recognition of human merit or goodness.

Perhaps a review would be helpful at this point. In Catholicism, justification is an internal renovation and empowering of man—both a regeneration and sanctification. It comes through an infusion of God's grace and it means that people, in their own being, are made just or pleasing to God. *The Catholic*

Encyclopedia offers the following as the definition of justification: "Primarily and simply justification is the possession of sanctifying grace....We are justified by Christ...and by good works...."[79]

According to Catholic teaching, justification is the gracious act of God whereby an individual—in cooperation with God—*makes himself righteous.*[80] Another way of saying this is that justification is the work of grace within a man which assists in making him internally and externally holy:

> ...the Bible shows that justification is a rebirth. It is a generation of a supernatural life in a former sinner (John 3:5; Titus 3:5), a thorough inner renewal (Ephesians 4:23), and a real sanctification (1 Corinthians 6:11). The soul itself becomes beautiful and holy. It is not just an ugly soul hidden under a beautiful cloak [a reference to the Protestant view of imputed righteousness]. Because it is beautiful and holy, it can be admitted to heaven where nothing unclean is allowed.[81]

Unfortunately, Catholicism has confused justification with sanctification and regeneration.[82] As Catholic P. Gregory Stevens writes in *The Life of Grace,* "First of all, justification is a real and profound transformation of man [regeneration], a genuine gift of sanctification to him."[83] But this is wrong because justification (Romans 3:28–4:6; Philippians 3:9), regeneration (John 3:6-7; 6:63; 2 Corinthians 5:17; Galatians 6:15), and sanctification (Ephesians 2:10; 2 Peter 3:18) are three distinct and separate biblical doctrines. To confuse them is to distort the very essence of biblical salvation.

The Bible teaches that justification is God's work of grace *in Christ* declaring the believer righteous. It is *not* God's work of grace *in man* to actually make him righteous, which is sanctification. (See Romans 10:1-4; 1 Corinthians 1:30.) The lexical documentation and discussion in footnote 75 proves the Catholic view of justification is wrong.

10
Do Protestants and Catholics now agree on the doctrine of justification, or are the teachings of the Council of Trent still authoritative?

In 1983 a group of Lutheran and Catholic theologians made the newsworthy announcement that they had come to agreement on the meaning of justification. Although this widely publicized statement caused many people to believe that Catholics and Protestants were now agreed on this doctrine, this was far from true.

First, whether or not some individual Catholic scholars accept the biblical doctrine of justification is not the same as having Rome accept it. Second, those involved did no such thing. Although their statement sounded evangelical, a careful reading of the report proves that what was upheld was the traditional Catholic doctrine of justification. For example, the report clearly equates justification and sanctification: "By justification we are both declared and made righteous. Justification, therefore, is not a legal fiction [a reference to the Protestant view]. God, in justifying, effects what He promises; He forgives sin and makes us truly righteous."[84]

But as W. Robert Godfrey, professor of church history at Westminster Theological Seminary in California, correctly observes, "The report yields to the Roman Catholics on the doctrine of justification, and compromises too much what is essential to the gospel."[85] Thus, the report did not unite Lutherans and Catholics on the nature of justification; it simply upheld the Catholic view. (See Question 14.) This unfortunate confusion has been repeated several times in the ensuing decades.

In essence, the decrees made by the Council of Trent on justification remain the standard of Roman Catholic theology. These decrees have never been modified, altered, or rescinded by Rome. This is why Karl Keating maintains that the views of Trent on justification are not only true Catholic doctrine, but that they are true biblical doctrine as well.[86]

The Catholic doctrine reiterated by the Council of Trent (1545–1563) is principally a reply to the "heresies" of the Protestant Reformation. A careful reading of the sixth session on justification will clearly show that, despite Catholic claims, its pronouncements are not only unbiblical, but anti-biblical as well.

Trent decreed that whoever does not "faithfully and firmly accept this Catholic doctrine on justification...cannot be justified...."[87] Thus, in the section "Canons Concerning Justification," we read:

> Canon 9—If anyone says that the sinner is justified by faith alone, meaning that nothing else is required to cooperate in order to obtain the grace of justification...let him be anathema [cursed by God].[88]

Not surprisingly, Trent also decreed that good works increase our justification. For example, in Canon 24:

> If anyone says that the justice received [i.e., justification] is not preserved and also not increased before God through good works, but that those works are merely the fruits and signs of justification obtained, but not the cause of its increase, let him be anathema.[89]

Trent establishes perhaps the most subtle form of justification by works ever devised. This subtlety may explain why some Catholics actively encourage Protestants to read the decrees of Trent—to "prove" that Catholicism does not teach a form of salvation by works. We do think that every Protestant should read these decrees *carefully* and then determine for themselves whether or not the gospel of grace has been rejected.

Because Roman Catholic teaching denies that justification is the past and completed declaration of God the Judge, it thoroughly undermines a believer's certainty of salvation. If "to justify" means to *make* a person righteous, a person is left to his own subjective condition for the basis of his acceptance before God. This explains why Catholic justification fluctuates in the life of a believer. It is *not* a completed act of God. Rather, it is based on the grace-empowered works of sinful people for its maintenance. Thus, it can hardly provide any sense of *security* of salvation. For example, since the Catholic Church teaches that justification can be lost by mortal sin, a person can only know he retains his justification if he is certain he has not committed mortal sin. But in Catholic teaching, such knowledge is problematic at best. Mortal sin is not always clearly defined,[90] so definite knowledge of having committed such a sin is not always possible.

Clearly, Catholics and Protestants are not in agreement on this vital matter of salvation.

11

How is the Roman Catholic view of biblical authority and inerrancy compromised?

Doctrinally, the Roman Catholic Church has traditionally taught that the Bible is the inerrant Word of God, and Catholics continue to maintain that they have the highest regard for Scripture. Rev. John A. O'Brien of Notre Dame University writes, "Far from being hostile to the Bible, the Catholic Church is its true mother....The simple fact is that the Catholic Church loves the Bible, reveres it as the inspired word of God, gives to it a loyalty and intelligent obedience greater than that of any other religious body in the world...—a loyalty of which history knows no parallel."[91]

But this position was compromised at Vatican II, which restricted biblical inerrancy to a more narrow spectrum of biblical teaching and also allowed for further encroachment of neoorthodoxy. In effect, the Church now holds to a position of "limited inerrancy": Scripture is inerrant, but not all of it.[92] (Exactly where it is and is not inerrant is left for the interpreter to decide, an example of "private judgment" the Church claims it rejects.)

Regardless, in practice, even the traditional view of inerrancy had long been compromised by 1) the Church's acceptance of the Apocrypha, 2) a belief in inerrant Tradition, and 3) the claim that the Church alone properly interprets Scripture.

1. The Apocrypha undermines inerrancy.

Catholicism teaches that Scripture involves more than the O.T. canon accepted by the Jews, Jesus, and the Church of the first four centuries, i.e., the 39 books of the Protestant Old Testament. It adds new portions to the books of Esther and Daniel plus seven additional books, which were written between the Testaments: Tobit, Judith, 1 and 2 Maccabees, Ben Sirach, (also called Ecclesiasticus), Baruch, and Wisdom.[93,94] The Catholic Church refers to these extra books as "deuterocanonical works"—those that are canonical or scriptural for Catholics but which were never part of the Jewish Bible.

The Apocrypha undermines a doctrine of inerrancy because these books contain historical and other errors. Thus, if the Apocrypha is considered Scripture, this identifies error with God's Word. This is why neither the Jews,[95] Jesus,[96] the apostles,[97] nor most of the early Church fathers[98] ever accepted the Apocrypha as Scripture.[99, cf. 100]

Biblical scholar Dr. Rene Pache comments, "Except for certain interesting historical information (especially in 1 Maccabees) and a few beautiful moral thoughts (e.g., Wisdom of Solomon), these books contain absurd legends and platitudes, and historical, geographical and chronological errors, as well as manifestly heretical doctrines; they even recommend immoral acts (Judith 9:10,13)."[101] Errors in the Apocrypha are frequently pointed out in standard works. For example,

> Tobit...contains certain historical and geographical errors such as the assumption that Sennacherib was the son of Shalmaneser (1:15) instead of Sargon II,

> and that Nineveh was captured by Nebuchadnezzar
> and Ahasuerus (14:5) instead of by Nabopolassar and
> Cyaxares....Judith cannot possibly be historical because
> of the glaring errors it contains....[In 2 Maccabees] there
> are also numerous disarrangements and discrepancies in
> chronological, historical, and numerical matters in the
> book, reflecting ignorance or confusion....[102]

For 1,500 years no Roman Catholic was required to believe that the Apocrypha was Scripture, until the Council of Trent made its fateful decree.[103] Unfortunately, the Council adopted its position "for reasons of expediency rather than evidence."[104] Thus, it was "unmindful of evidence, of former popes and scholars, of the Fathers of the church and the witness of Christ and the apostles" in making its decision to include the Apocrypha as Scripture.[105]

Dr. Pache points out that one of the reasons Trent accepted the Apocrypha was merely in response to the arguments of the Reformers who were attempting to defend the principle of "sola scriptura"—that the Bible alone is the believer's authority.

> Why, then, did Rome take so new and daring a position? Because, confronted by the Reformers, she lacked arguments to justify her unscriptural deviations. She declared that the Apocryphal books supported such doctrines as prayers for dead (II Maccabees 12:44); the expiatory sacrifice (eventually to become the Mass, II Maccabees 12:39-46); alms giving with expiatory value, also leading to deliverance from death (Tobit 12:9; 4:10); invocation and intercession of the saints (II Maccabees 15:14; Bar. 3:4); the worship of angels (Tobit 12:12); purgatory; and the redemption of souls after death (II Maccabees 12:42,46).[106]

2. Catholic Tradition undermines inerrancy.

As noted before, Catholicism accepts sacred Tradition as having divine authority: Vatican II emphasized that Catholic Scripture and Tradition "form one sacred deposit of the word of God."[107] Thus, "both Sacred Tradition and Sacred Scripture are to be accepted and venerated with the same sense of loyalty and reverence."[108] Karl Keating thinks that "...the trouble of [the] fundamentalist [e.g., evangelical] is that he labors under the misconception that Scripture has the last word…" and that Tradition "counts for nothing."[109]

Of course, biblically, there is nothing wrong with tradition. Even Scripture acknowledges its usefulness, but only when it is based upon apostolic teaching (e.g., 2 Thessalonians 2:15; 3:6) or not in conflict with Scripture itself. When tradition reflects the truths of Scripture, this is fine. But when it denies and opposes God's word in the Bible, we have a problem.

Catholic Tradition comprises a massive body of literature—the teachings of the early Fathers, historic creeds, the writings of Church scholars and leaders, laws given by synods and councils, papal decrees, etc. Today, one of the Catholic Church's normal functions is to continue this refinement of doctrine and practice.

Several problems are created by the Church's claim that this mass of data is, in some sense, necessary for salvation and/or infallible. First, there is the insuperable difficulty in authoritatively determining where infallible Tradition lies. As Keating confesses, "The big problem, no doubt, is determining what constitutes authentic tradition."[110] Second, the large amount of data itself poses a problem. Papal "Bulls," or written communications from or authorized by the pope, from 450–1850 alone comprise more than 40 volumes. This has led to "almost inextricable difficulties" for Catholic theologians.[111] Third, problems relating to the fact of errors, demonstrable self-contradictions, and even denials of biblical teaching are inescapable. Fourth, contradictory Tradition and differences in the historical *interpretation* of Tradition have plagued the claim to infallibility. For example, even popes have disagreed on such subjects as religious freedom, the validity of civil marriages, the legitimacy of Bible reading, the order of the Jesuits, Galileo's scientific data, and other topics.[112] On rare occasion, popes have even sided with heresy, as did Pope Liberius (reigned from 352 to 366) when he accepted the Arians who rejected Christ's deity (cf.

Zozimus and the Pelagians, Honorius I and the Monothelites, or Vigilius and the Monphysites and Nestorians).

Finally, when any other source of authority is put on par with Scripture, Scripture usually becomes secondary. According to Keating, "Fundamentalists say the Bible is the sole rule of faith....Catholics, on the other hand, say the Bible is not the sole rule of faith and that nothing in the Bible suggests it was meant to be."[113] However, "we need only read Church history to discover that when another source of authority is placed alongside Scripture as of equal importance, Scripture eventually becomes relegated to the background."[114]

If Catholic Tradition were, in fact, "inerrant" and "sacred," then it would not deny Scripture.[115] Perhaps this explains why many of the Church's unscriptural doctrines were added in the midst of debate and dissension among Catholics themselves. For example, at the Council of Trent not all participants thought it credible that the Apocrypha was Scripture. And, at the first Vatican council, not all present believed the Pope should be considered infallible.[116]

3. Catholic interpretation undermines inerrancy.

In *The Documents of Vatican II*, under the category of "Revelation," we find the following:

> The task of authentically interpreting the word of God, whether written or handed on [i.e., Tradition], has been entrusted *exclusively* to the living, teaching office of the Church....[117]

The Catholic Church allocates to itself the sole power to properly interpret the Catholic Bible and Tradition. The Protestant view of an individual's right to devoutly interpret the Bible by diligent study (2 Timothy 2:15) and under the illumination of the Holy Spirit is rejected as false.[118]

Keating claims that the evangelicals' understanding of the Bible as the sole authority is irrational because "the individual is the least solid of all

46

interpreters." He believes the only manner in which we can know the Bible really is inspired is if an infallible Church tells us it is.[119]

Of course, we must ask the question—is the Catholic Church truly infallible? Is its Tradition inerrant? Does it always interpret the Bible correctly? It claims so. This is why Keating and other Catholics refer to "the authoritative and infallible Church" and "the fact of an infallible teaching Church."[120] But where is the evidence?

It is important here to understand what the Catholic Church means by infallible. Infallibility is officially defined as "immunity from error, excluding not only its existence, but even its possibility."[121] This infallibility extends not only to the Pope in matters of faith and morals, but also to the bishops in teaching and, by implication, interpretation.[122] But, as history proves, the Roman Catholic Church has not been infallible—despite its claims. As Hans Kung, a well-respected but dissident Catholic theologian, points out, "The errors of the Ecclesiastical teaching office in every generation have been numerous and indisputable....And yet the teaching office constantly found it difficult to admit these errors frankly and honestly...."[123]

Consider a modern example. Most Catholic literature contains the *Nihil Obstat* and the *Imprimature*, Church seals that designate authority. They are defined as a "declaration that a book or pamphlet is considered to be free from doctrinal or moral error."[124] Yet *The Catholic Encyclopedia*, which contains these seals, teaches the following demonstrable errors:

1. Salvation is by works (and other theological errors)

2. Muslims worship the biblical God

3. The book of Daniel was written in 165 B.C.

4. Mormons "believe in the Trinity"

5. Papal infallibility is true

6. The Catholic Church is the only true Church

The Catholic Encyclopedia also includes positive reviews of the Hindu practice of Transcendental Meditation, the religion of Islam, and the destructive approach to Scripture known as Form Criticism.[125] Such teachings indicate that *The Catholic Encyclopedia* is not free from doctrinal and spiritual errors.

Books such as Karl Keating's *Catholicism and Fundamentalism*, which seek to critique evangelical Christianity from the perspective of Catholic dogma, have this problem in common: Catholic doctrine *precedes* exegesis. The Bible is interpreted primarily in light of Church doctrine and not its own teachings. Where the Bible conflicts with Catholic dogma, no appeal to Scripture is sufficient because in the end, Scripture is not the final authority—only what the Church interprets and teaches is the final authority.

The fact that "infallible" popes have consistently upheld unbiblical Roman Catholic doctrine proves that it is Catholic doctrine derived from Tradition which interprets the Bible, and not standard principles of exegesis.[126]

In other words, while Tradition has authority over Scripture, the teaching office of the Church has authority over Tradition because it decides what Tradition is (and thus what Scripture is) and how to properly interpret them both.[127] This is why Catholics hold that it is their Tradition that "gives life to Scripture."[128]

This also tells us why, in a very real sense, Church Tradition is considered necessary for salvation: "Magisterium of the Church is the power given by Christ to the Church together with infallibility by which the Church teaches authoritatively the revealed truth of the Scripture *and holds forth the truth of tradition for salvation.*"[129]

Unfortunately, Rome has left her Church without the divinely given means to determine truth from error—namely the inerrant authority of the Scriptures alone.[130] The Church itself becomes the standard of truth in whatever it teaches or does, and thus there is no higher authority to which it must submit or standard by which it must be judged.[131]

In conclusion, by 1) adding the errant Apocrypha to the canon, 2) accepting errant Tradition as divine revelation, 3) claiming that proper interpretation of Scripture/Tradition resides only in the Catholic Church, and 4) asserting infallibility for itself, the Catholic Church has effectively undermined the inerrancy and authority of the Bible.

12

Is the Pope infallible?

The Catholic Church teaches that when the Pope speaks "ex cathedra" (i.e., "from his chair" or authoritatively[132]), he is infallible in matters of faith and morals.

Papal infallibility was officially defined and promulgated on July 18, 1870 at the first Vatican Council.[133] What this means is that for 1,870 years the Catholic Church did *not* officially teach that the Pope was infallible. Even within the Council itself, there were many protests, and a large number of other faithful Catholics rejected it as well, earning for themselves the title "Old Catholics."[134]

We grant that most papal statements are not made under the strictures of the 1870 *ex cathedra* definition. But that is not the issue. Rather, the issue is that such pronouncements in general uphold the *doctrinal* position of Catholicism overall.

A thorough discussion of the Vatican I Council can be found in August Bernard Hasler's *How the Pope Became Infallible*. Hasler served for five years in the Vatican Secretariat for Christian Unity where he was given access to the Vatican Archives. There he uncovered crucial documents relating to the council that had never been studied before. As a result of his research, this learned Catholic scholar concluded:

It is becoming increasingly obvious, in fact, that the dogma of papal infallibility has no basis either in the Bible or the history of the Church during the first millennium. If, however, the First Vatican Council was not free, then neither was it ecumenical. And in that case its decrees have no claim to validity. So the way is clear to revise this Council and, at the same time, to escape from a situation which both history and theology find more and more indefensible. Is this asking too much of the Church? Can it ever admit that a council erred, that in 1870 Vatican I made the wrong decision?[135]

Papal infallibility has never been a credible doctrine. As Carson points out in his study of contemporary Catholicism, the doctrine of an infallible Pope and/or Church reasonably assumes that the infallible guide will first of all be clearly recognizable; second, that this guide will act with reasonable promptitude in discerning truth from error; and third, that this guide can *never* be responsible for leading the Church into error.[136] But in the history of the Catholic Church, this has not been the case.

13

What is the unique role of Mary in Roman Catholicism, and is it biblical?

Significant areas of Catholic doctrine and practice are related to the person and work of Mary. Her unique relationship to God is usually discussed in a trinity of functions: 1) *Co-redemptrix*, 2) *Mediatrix*, and 3) *Queen of Heaven*. As Co-redemptrix, she cooperates with Christ in the work of saving sinners. As Mediatrix, she dispenses God's blessings and grace to the spiritually needy. As Queen of Heaven, she rules providentially with Christ, the King of Heaven.[137] Although views in the Roman Church vary, Mary has usually been elevated above all the prophets, apostles, saints, popes, and even the Catholic Church itself. In the words of Pope Paul VI, "...The place she occupies in the Church [is] 'the highest place and the closest to us after Jesus.'"[138]

With the honored blessing given by Vatican II,[139] Mariology is as firmly entrenched in Catholicism as ever. Vatican II declares: "It admonishes all the sons of the Church that the cult, especially the liturgical cult, of the Blessed Virgin, be generously fostered."[140] But the Catholic view of Mary is not scriptural; to the contrary, it is entirely traditional. Some of the unbiblical teachings relating to the Mary of Catholic Tradition include the following:

1. *Mary's immaculate conception:* She was born without original sin and was, therefore, sinless throughout her life.

2. *Mary's perpetual virginity:* She had no children after Jesus.

3. *Mary's bodily assumption or physical ascension into heaven:* Because of her sinlessness, Mary never experienced physical death. She was raised bodily into the presence of Christ.

4. *Mary as Co-redemptrix and Mediatrix of all graces:* The obedience and sufferings of Mary were essential to secure the full redemption bought by Christ.

5. *Mary's right to veneration and/or worship:* Because of her unparalleled role in the economy of salvation, Mary is worthy of special adoration.

Space permits discussion of only these last two points.

Is Mary a "Savior"?

Mariology is defined as the study of that theology "which treats the life, role and virtues of the Blessed Mother of God" and which "demonstrates...her position as Co-redemptrix and Mediatrix of all graces."[141] Thus, Catholic popes have always glorified Mary.

Pope Leo XIII stated in his rosary encyclical, "Octobri mense" (1891): *"Nobody can approach Christ except through the mother."*[142] Pope Pius X (1903–1914) asserted that Mary is "the dispenser of all gifts which Jesus has acquired for us by His death and His blood."[143] Pope Pius XI (1922–1939) says, "With Jesus, Mary has redeemed the human race."[144] The conclusion of Pope Pius XII (1939–1958) in his encyclical, "Mystici Corporis" (1943), was that Mary willingly offered Christ on Golgotha: "Who, free from all sin, original or personal, and always most intimately united with her Son, offered him on Golgotha to the eternal Father...for all the children of Adam."[145]

All this is why Vatican II declared that, "Taken up to heaven, she did not lay aside this saving role, but by her manifold acts of intercession continued to win for us gifts of eternal salvation."*[146] And in *The Catholic Response*, Stravinskas remarks that, "One cannot ignore this woman, lest one risk distorting the gospel itself."[147, cf. 148]

Although Mary did not literally die for the sin of the world, by giving birth to the Messiah and by giving Him moral support and other things, Mary can be seen as *indirectly* helping to atone for the sins of the world. Thus, of her temporal earthly sufferings, *The Catholic Encyclopedia* teaches that she "endured them for our salvation."[149] Further, "in the power of the grace of Redemption merited by Christ, Mary, by her spiritual entering into the sacrifice of her Divine Son for men, *made atonement for the sins of men* and (*de congruon*) merited the application of the redemptive grace of Christ. In this manner she cooperates in the subjective redemption of mankind."[150]

---

* The "maximalists" assert that by means of her Fiat and offering of her Son on the cross Mary is absolutely necessary not only to the Incarnation but to Redemption itself. This is why she is called a Co-redemptrix. But even the so-called "minimalists" affirm such beliefs as Mary's alleged bodily assumption, immaculate conception, and her coronation as Queen of Heaven.

Is Mary Worshiped?

Although Catholic theology attempts to draw a line between the worship offered to God and that offered to Mary, in practice these frequently become indistinguishable.

> Rome may deny that Mary is worshiped as God. But to attribute to her powers which involve omniscience and omnipresence, if she is to hear [and answer] the prayers of millions, is to accord to her what belongs to God alone. Furthermore, the prayers themselves are phrased in such a way that it is hard to distinguish them from those offered to God.[151]

Pope John Paul II (1920–) chose *totus tuus* ("I am completely yours, O Mary") as the motto for his papacy. In his book *Crossing the Threshold of Hope*, the Pope explains:

> *Totus Tuus.* This phrase is not only an expression of piety, or simply an expression of devotion. It is more. During the Second World War, while I was employed as a factory worker, I came to be attracted to Marian devotion. At first, it had seemed to me that I should distance myself a bit from the Marian devotion of my childhood, in order to focus more on Christ. Thanks to Saint Louis of Montfort, I came to understand that true *devotion to the Mother of God is actually Christo-centric, indeed, it is very profoundly rooted in the Mystery of the Blessed Trinity*, and the mysteries of the Incarnation and Redemption.[152]

On May 13, 1981, Pope John Paul II was severely wounded by a gunman. Bleeding profusely, the Pope lost consciousness, quickly, but not before crying out, "Mary, my Mother." According to author Tad Szulc the Pope believes his life was saved as a "real miracle" by the Virgin of Fatima. John Paul II went to her shrine on the first anniversary of the attack to thank the Virgin for saving him and to offer to her the bullet that nearly killed him.[153] That day the Pope gave an Act of Consecration to Mary, which included:

Immaculate Heart! Help us to conquer the menace of evil...From famine and war, deliver us....From sins against the life of man from its very beginning, deliver us. From hatred and from the demeaning of the dignity of the children of God, deliver us. From every kind of injustice in the life of society, both national and international, deliver us. From readiness to trample on the commandments of God, deliver us. From attempts to stifle in human hearts the very truth of God, deliver us. From the loss of awareness of evil, deliver us. From sins against the Holy Spirit, deliver us.[154]

Again, the Catholic Church officially claims that its Mariology does not subtract from the worship due Christ as God and Mediator.[155] But as you've seen, this doesn't seem to be true.

The Biblical Mary

The Mary of Catholic teaching has little to do with the Mary of the New Testament. Given Mary's supreme importance in the Catholic Church, it's amazing to consider the complete absence of even the mention of her name in the New Testament epistles.

Apart from Acts 1:14, Mary is mentioned nowhere else outside the Gospels. And even in the Gospels, her spiritual power and authority are almost nonexistent. Neither Jesus Christ, nor Paul, nor any other biblical writer ever gave Mary the place or devotion the Catholic Church has given her for a thousand years. This is all the more incredible when we consider that the New Testament letters were written specifically for the spiritual guidance of the church, and they have a great deal to say about both doctrine and worship. Even Catholics are forced to confess that scriptural support for these doctrines is lacking.[156]

The apostle Luke relates an interesting incident in the life of Jesus. In effect, the story tells us that apart from her role as bearer and mother of the Messiah, Mary was not unique or especially blessed: "...One of the women in the crowd raised her voice, and said to Him, 'Blessed is the womb that bore You, and the breasts at which You nursed.' But He said, 'On the contrary, blessed are those who hear the word of God, and observe it'" (Luke 11:27-28 NASB). Jesus often referred to Himself as "the Son of Man," but never once, as Catholics do, as "the Son of Mary."

14

Can the differences between Catholics and Evangelicals be set aside?

In 1994 prominent members of Protestant and Catholic churches wrote and endorsed "Evangelicals & Catholics Together: The Christian Mission in the Third Millennium." Emphasizing Christian unity and tolerance, this document minimized the differences between Roman Catholicism and traditional Christianity to the point that Catholic doctrines could be interpreted as minor variances to biblical teachings:

> First...we as Evangelicals and Catholics affirm that opportunity and means for growth in Christian discipleship are available in our several communities. Second, the decision of the committed Christian with respect to his communal allegiance and participation must be assiduously respected. Third, in view of the larger number of non-Christians in the world and the enormous challenge of our common evangelistic task, *it is neither theologically legitimate nor a prudent use of resources for one Christian community to proselytize among active adherents of another Christian community....*Also to be rejected is the practice of comparing the strengths and ideals of one community with the weaknesses and failures of another....[157]

Although the document acknowledges several major differences between Catholicism and Protestantism, it goes on to say:

> These differing beliefs...should be honestly presented to the Christian who has undergone conversion. But

again, his decision regarding communal allegiance and participation must be assiduously respected....[He is] ultimately responsible to God, and *we dare not interfere with the exercise of that responsibility*.

The Protestant signers of the document seem to be saying that as long as people acknowledge God and His Son Jesus, it doesn't matter what they believe or practice. The fact that Roman Catholicism teaches the need for a pope and priests to intercede on behalf of the people; the Church is the only entity that accurately interprets Scriptures; Mary should be prayed to and is essential to salvation; and the pope infallibly represents and speaks for God appears inconsequential!*

As we've pointed out, there are critical differences between Catholicism and traditional Christianity. But still the convergence of these two belief systems is subtly promoted. "At the 1996 Charlotte Crusade held by Evangelist Billy Graham, the decision cards of 1700 Catholic responders to his invitation to commit their lives to Christ were given to the local Catholic Diocese for follow up."[158] As much as we respect and appreciate Billy Graham's ministry, it's not spiritually productive that seekers of biblical truth would be guided to the Catholic Church for godly advice and teaching.

This is not to say that the Catholic Church is devoid of genuine Christians—there are many. The real question, though, is one of commitment to biblical truth and the importance of spiritual growth based on it. The issue then becomes, "Can Christians remain in the Catholic Church without compromising their faith and/or their spiritual growth?"

We can hardly say that God would never allow Christians to remain in the Catholic Church in order to lead others to personal faith in Christ. But in order to do so effectively, these believers have to be thoroughly informed on the issues, weighing them carefully, resolving not to partake in practices or to accept

---

* After an outcry from Protestant conservatives, signers of the ECT issued clarifying statements January 1995 and January 1998.

doctrines that are not biblical. Further, we would sus-
pect that for the vast majority of Christians in the
Catholic Church, acquiring such discernment may
necessitate a lengthy absence from Rome.

Thus, we think it prudent for Catholics who
receive Christ as their personal Savior to find a place
where they can receive biblical teaching and Christian fellowship that will encourage their commitment to Christ and His Word alone. Once grounded
in those beliefs, a program of closer ministry to Rome
may be possible.

A PERSONAL WORD
TO CATHOLICS

If you have stayed with us this far, we want you to know we appreciate your perseverance and your integrity in examining a critique of the faith you hold dear. We have written this book because we believe there is one vital issue that all Catholics need to think through: personal salvation.

Catholics, perhaps more than anyone else, believe that it is not possible in this life to have assurance of salvation (except perhaps in very rare circumstances). You have been taught that the belief in the assurance of salvation is a "presumption upon the mercy of God"[159] and that mortal sin results in "eternal separation from God," requiring penance for restoration.[160] You have heard about the personal hazards of "triumphalism," something that arises from an "assurance of having been saved," which is a dangerous position to hold.[161] But the "assurance of having been saved" is a *biblical* doctrine, as 1 John 5:13 proves: "I write these things to you who believe in the name of the Son of God so that you may know that you have eternal life."

You also know that because Catholicism teaches that a Christian may lose his or her salvation, it argues that "not even faith…or conversion…or reception of baptism…or constancy throughout life…can gain for one the right to salvation…" and that all these are held to be only "the forerunners of attainment" toward salvation.[162]

But again, this is not biblical teaching. Jesus taught that faith does bring the right to salvation: "As many as received Him, to them He gave *the right* to become children of God" (John 1:12, NASB, emphasis added). The Bible clearly teaches that by faith alone people can know they are eternally saved because they, at the moment of saving faith, possess eternal life. You can know this by truly trusting in Christ for forgiveness of sins and making Him your personal Savior.

57

If you are a Catholic and desire to receive Jesus Christ as your personal Lord and Savior, we urge you to say the following prayer:

> *Dear God, it is my desire to enter into a personal relationship with You through the death of Your Son Jesus Christ on the cross. Although I have believed many things about Jesus, I confess that I have never truly received Him individually as my personal Savior and Lord. I have never realized that salvation was a gift that You offer me freely. I now receive that gift and believe that Christ died on the cross for my sins—all of them. I believe that He rose from the dead. It is my desire that He now become my Lord and Savior and so, I now receive Him into my life. I make Him Lord over all areas of my life, including any personal beliefs or practices that are not biblical.*
>
> *Help me to be committed to study Your Word and to grow as a Christian in ways that honor You. Give me the strength to face difficulty or rejection when it comes to making a stand for You. If it is Your will and necessary for me to leave this Church, guide me into a good church and fellowship so that I might know and glorify You more. In Jesus' name I pray this, trusting in Your guidance. Amen.*

NOTES

1. Robert C. Broderick, ed., *The Catholic Encyclopedia,* revised and updated (Nashville: Thomas Nelson Publishers, 1987), 597.
2. As quoted by Karl Keating, *Catholicism and Fundamentalism: The Attack on "Romanism" by "Bible Christians"* (San Francisco: Ignatius Press, 1988), 150.
3. Emmett McLoughlin, *Crime and Immorality in the Catholic Church* (New York: Lyle Stuart, 1964), 19.
4. Broderick, ed., *Catholic Encyclopedia,* 73-74.
5. Ibid., 581.
6. Ibid., 292.
7. Ibid.
8. Ibid., 581.
9. Norman Geisler and William Nix, *A General Introduction to the Bible* (Chicago, IL: Moody Press, 1971), 62, 66.
10. Ibid., 87; cf. Romans 3:2; 2 Timothy 3:15; 2 Peter 1:20-21.
11. Ibid., 88.
12. Ibid., 91, 97. Examples of New Testament claims for divine inspiration include Hebrews 1:1-2; 1 Corinthians 2:1,7,10,12-13; Galatians 1:11-12; Ephesians 5:26; 1 Thessalonians 2:13; 4:8; James 1:18; 1 Peter 1:25; 2 Peter 3:2,16; 1 Timothy 4:1; Revelation 1:1-3; 22:18-19.
13. As quoted by Harold Lindsell, *The Battle for the Bible* (Grand Rapids, MI: Zondervan Publishing House, 1977), 67.
14. J. Barton Payne, *The Encyclopedia of Biblical Prophecy* (Grand Rapids, MI: Baker Book House, 1989), passim; John Ankerberg, *The Case for Jesus the Messiah* (Eugene, OR: Harvest House Publishers, 1989), passim.
15. John Ankerberg, *Do the Resurrection Accounts Conflict? And What Proof Is There That Jesus Rose from the Dead?* (Chattanooga, TN: Ankerberg Theological Research Institute, 1989), passim. See also Colossians 1:13-23; John 2:19.
16. E.g., John Wenham, *Christ and the Bible* (Downers Grove, IL: InterVarsity Press, 1973), chapters 1-2, 5; also his chapter in *Inerrancy,* Norman L. Geisler, ed. (Grand Rapids, MI: Zondervan Publishing House, 1980), 3-38; Pierre C.H. Marcel, "Our Lord's Use of Scripture" in *Revelation and the Bible,* Carl Henry, ed. (Grand Rapids, MI: Baker Book House, 1969), 119-134; Rene Pache, *The Inspiration and Authority of Scripture* (Chicago, IL: Moody Press, 1969), chapter 18.
17. Lausanne Committee for World Evangelization, "Christian Witness to Nominal Christians Among Roman Catholics," The Thailand Report on Roman Catholics (Wheaton, IL: Lausanne Committee, 1980), 10.
18. Broderick, ed., *Catholic Encyclopedia,* 372.
19. Keating, *Catholicism and Fundamentalism,* 103.
20. Paul G. Schrotenboer, ed., *Roman Catholicism: A Contemporary Evangelical Perspective* (Grand Rapids, MI: Baker Book House, 1980), 7.
21. Ibid.
22. John Phillips, "Can a Christian Remain a Roman Catholic?" *Moody Monthly* (April 1982), 31.
23. Millard J. Erickson, *Christian Theology* (Grand Rapids, MI: Baker Book House, 1986), 901.
24. H.M. Carson, *Dawn or Twilight? A Study of Contemporary Roman Catholicism* (Leicester, England: InterVarsity Press, 1976).
25. Broderick, ed., *Catholic Encyclopedia,* 246.
26. Ibid., 253.
27. Ibid., 65.
28. Ibid., 131.

29. Ibid., 466-468, 319.
30. Ibid., 375-376.
31. Ibid., 372.
32. Ibid., 39-40, 208.
33. Ibid., 438-439.
34. H.J. Schroeder, trans., *The Canons and Decrees of the Council of Trent* (Rockford, IL: Tan Books, 1978), 7th Session, Canon 1, 51.
35. Ibid., 7th Session, Canon 4, 52.
36. Ibid., 53.
37. As quoted by the *Los Angeles Times* (March 8, 1983), Part I, 10.
38. Editorial, "What Separates Evangelicals and Catholics?" *Christianity Today* (October 23, 1981), 14-15, emphasis added.
39. Anne Fremantle, *The Papal Encyclicals in Their Historical Context: The Teachings of the Popes* (New York: New American Library/Mentor, 1956), 11.
40. Keating, *Catholicism and Fundamentalism*, 81.
41. Schroeder, *Canons and Decrees*, 42.
42. Fremantle, *Papal Encyclicals*, 18.
43. Martin Chemnitz, *Examination of the Council of Trent*, Fred Kramer, trans. (St. Louis, MO: Concordia Publishing House, 1978), Part 1, 213.
44. Ludwig Ott, *Fundamentals of Catholic Dogma* (Rockford, IL: Tan Books, 1974), 340-341, emphasis added.
45. John Hardon, *The Catholic Catechism: The Contemporary Catechism of the Teachings of the Catholic Church* (Garden City, NY: Doubleday, 1975), 506-507.
46. Rod Rosenblad and Karl Keating, "The Salvation Debate," conducted at Simon Greenleaf School of Law (March 11, 1989), cassette tape.
47. Ibid.
48. Broderick, ed., *Catholic Encyclopedia*, 65, emphasis added.
49. Ibid., 254.
50. Ibid.
51. Ibid., 105.
52. Ibid., 466; cf. Ott, *Fundamentals of Catholic Dogma*, 425.
53. Broderick, ed., *Catholic Encyclopedia*, 467.
54. Schroeder, *Canons and Decrees*, 14th Session, Canon 2, 102.
55. Schrotenboer, ed., *Roman Catholicism: A Contemporary Evangelical Perspective*, 68-69, citing the encyclical *Ad Catholic sacerdotii*, 1935, and Pope Paul VI in *Mysterium fidei*, no. 38.
56. Ott, *Fundamentals of Catholic Dogma*, 431, emphasis added.
57. As quoted by Keating, *Catholicism and Fundamentalism*, 248, emphasis added.
58. Hardon, *Catholic Catechism*, 468, emphasis added.
59. Ott, *Fundamentals of Catholic Dogma*, 407.
60. Hardon, 413.
61. Broderick, ed., *Catholic Encyclopedia*, 285, emphasis added.
62. Pope Paul VI, *Devotion to the Blessed Virgin Mary* (Washington, D.C.: United States Catholic Conference, Publications Office, 1974), 37, Apostolic Exhortation *Marialis Cultus*.
63. Ott, *Fundamentals of Catholic Dogma*, 412.
64. The Daughters of St. Paul, *The Christ of Vatican II* (Boston: Daughters of St. Paul, 1968), 12, 15-16, emphasis added.
65. Pope Paul VI, *Devotion to the Blessed Virgin Mary*, 37.
66. St. Louis De Montfort, *The Secret of the Rosary*, Mary Barbour, trans. (Bay Shore, NY: Montfort Publications, 1976), 65.
67. Broderick, ed., *Catholic Encyclopedia*, 117.
68. Ott, *Fundamentals of Catholic Dogma*, 485.
69. Hardon, *Catholic Catechism*, 273.
70. Ibid., 274.

71. Ibid., 263-274.

72. Ibid., 274.

73. Broderick, ed., *Catholic Encyclopedia*, 502, emphasis added.

74. Keating, *Catholicism and Fundamentalism*, 166-168, 175, emphasis added.

75. Catholic theologians claim that Paul's use of *dikaioo* does not refer to *imputed* righteousness. But they did not get this from standard Greek dictionaries which define the principal New Testament word for justification (*dikaioo*; cf. Luke 18:14; Romans 3:24-28; 4:5; 5:1,9; 8:30,33; 1 Corinthians 6:11; Galatians 2:16; 3:8,11,24; Titus 3:7) in a Protestant and *not* a Catholic sense—as a legal declaration of righteousness, not an infusing of actual righteousness. As the premier Greek lexicon puts it, "In Paul, the legal usage is plain and indisputable....[It] does not suggest the infusion of moral qualities...[but] the justification of the ungodly who believe...the result of a judicial pronouncement" (Gerhard Kittel, ed., *Theological Dictionary of the New Testament*, Vol. 2, 215-216). Thus, if the believer actually possesses the righteousness of Christ by divine decree, it can hardly be a "legal fiction," as Catholics maintain who think that to declare sinners righteous is inconsistent with God's justice. But God says that it is His *imputing* of righteousness to the *sinner* that proves He *is* just (Romans 3:26) (cf. *The Hebrew Greek Study Bible*, [1984,23]: "to render just or innocent"; Arndt and Gingrich [1967,196]: "being acquitted, be pronounced and treated as righteous"; *New Thayers' Greek-English Lexicon* [1977,150]: "which never means to *make* worthy, but to judge worthy, to declare worthy...to declare guiltless...to judge, declare, pronounce righteous and therefore acceptable"; Loruv and Nida's *Greek-English Lexicon* [1988,557]: "the act of clearing someone of transgression—'to acquit, to set free, to remove guilt, acquittal.' " This is why Bruce Metzger, perhaps the premier Greek scholar in America, emphasizes it is "past comprehension" how someone can deny "the unmistakable evidence" of the Pauline meaning of this word: "The fact is that Paul simply does not use this verb to mean 'to be made upright or righteous.' Indeed, it is extremely doubtful whether it ever bore this meaning in the Greek of any period or author....It means 'to be pronounced, or declared, or treated as righteous or upright.' " Noted theologian J.I. Packer says, "There is no lexical grounds for the view of...the medieval and Roman theologians that 'justify' means or connotes as part of its meaning 'making righteous' by subjective spiritual renewal. The tridentine [Council of Trent] definition of justification as not only the remission of sins but also the sanctification and renewal of the inward man is erroneous." (Statements by Bruce Metzger and J.I. Packer taken from Rosenblad and Keating, "The Salvation Debate," March 11, 1989.)

76. As cited in "The Basic Catholic Doctrine of Justification by Faith," *Present Truth: Special Issue—Justification by Faith*, Robert D. Brinsmead, ed. (P.O. Box 1311, Fallbrook, California 92028), n.d., 7.

77. R.C. Sproul, "Systematic Theology," transcribed lecture (1987), 6.

78. Keating in "The Salvation Debate" (March 11, 1989).

79. Broderick, ed., *Catholic Encyclopedia*, 319.

80. Brinsmead, ed., *Present Truth*, 8.

81. Keating, *Catholicism and Fundamentalism*, 168.

82. Schroeder, *Canons and Decrees*, 29-46, 6th Session, canons on justification.

83. As quoted by Brinsmead, ed., *Present Truth*, 8.

84. As quoted by W. Robert Godfrey, "Reversing the Reformation," *Eternity* (Sept. 1984), 28.

85. Ibid., 27.

86. Keating in "The Salvation Debate" (March 11, 1989).

87. Schroeder, *Canons and Decrees*, 42.

88. Ibid., 43.

89. Ibid., 45.

90. Broderick, ed., *Catholic Encyclopedia*, 402.

91. Rev. John A. O'Brien, *The Faith of Millions* (Huntington, IN: Our Sunday Visitor, 1974), 126.

92. Wells, *Revolution in Rome*, 29-31.

93. Broderick, ed., *Catholic Encyclopedia*, 160.

94. Keating, *Catholicism and Fundamentalism*, 46.

95. Cf. D.G. Dunbar in D.A. Carson and John D. Woodbridge, eds., *Hermeneutics, Authority, and Canon* (Grand Rapids, MI: Zondervan Publishing House, 1986), 309-310; cf. F.F. Bruce, *The Canon of Scripture* (Downers Grove, IL: InterVarsity Press, 1988), 34, 41-42.

96. R. Laird Harris, *Inspiration and Canonicity of the Bible: An Historical and Exegetical Study* (Grand Rapids, MI: Zondervan Publishing House, 1973), 184; cf. F.F. Bruce, *Canon of Scripture*, 27-28, 41-42, 255, 260.

97. Pache, *Inspiration and Authority*, 172.

98. Harris, *Inspiration and Canonicity*, 188-191.

99. See note 103.

100. Harris, *Inspiration and Canonicity*, 137-138; cf. Proverbs 30:5-6; Deuteronomy 4:2; Revelation 22:18.

101. Pache, *Inspiration and Authority*, 172.

102. *Zondervan Pictorial Encyclopedia of the Bible*, Vol. 1, 207-210; cf. the discussion in Geisler and Nix, *A General Introduction*, 167-177 and *Encyclopedia Britannica*, Macropaedia, Vol. 2, 932ff.

103. See Bernard Ramm, *Protestant Christian Evidences* (Chicago, IL: Moody Press, 1971), 20. In his article, "The Apocrypha," *Kings Business* (July 1947), 15-17, he discusses many reasons why it is impossible to accept the Apocrypha as Scripture.

104. Harris, *Inspiration and Canonicity*, 193.

105. Ibid., 192.

106. Pache, *Inspiration and Authority*, 173.

107. Walter M. Abbott, general editor, *The Documents of Vatican II* (New York: Guild Press, 1966), 117.

108. Hardon, *Catholic Catechism*, 47 citing Second Vatican Council, *Dogmatic Constitution on Divine Revelation*, II, 9.

109. Keating, *Catholicism and Fundamentalism*, 151.

110. Ibid., 139.

111. General Legislation of the New Code of Canon Law, 71, cited in Richard Knolls, *Roman Catholicism: Issues and Evidences* (Chattanooga, TN: The John Ankerberg Show), n.d.

112. John Weldon, *Roman Catholicism Today* (ms., 1992); cf. Henry T. Hudson, *Papal Power: Its Origins and Development* (Hertfordshire, England: Evangelical Press, 1983), 112; Dreyer and Weller, *Roman Catholicism in the Light of Scripture* (Chicago, IL: Moody Press, 1960), 13-16; H.M. Carson, *Dawn or Twilight?* 80-85; Knolls, *Roman Catholicism: Issues and Evidences*, passim and Gregory XVI's *Mirari Vos* (1832).

113. Keating, *Catholicism and Fundamentalism*, 134.

114. Loraine Boettner, *Roman Catholicism* (Philadelphia, PA: Presbyterian and Reformed Publishing Company, 1973), 89.

115. Phillips, "Can a Christian Remain a Catholic?" 31-32; cf. Broderick, ed., *Catholic Encyclopedia*, 56, 285, 292, 365, 529 for examples.

116. Geisler and Nix, *A General Introduction*, 176; Broderick, ed., *Catholic Encyclopedia*, 434.

117. Abbott, ed., *Documents of Vatican II*, 117-118, emphasis added.

118. E.g., Keating, *Catholicism and Fundamentalism*, 82, 141.

119. Ibid., 20, 82, 126-127.

120. Ibid., 20, 132.

121. Hardon, *Catholic Catechism*, 224.

122. Hans Kung, *Infallible? An Inquiry* (Garden City, NY: Doubleday/Image, 1972), 60.
123. Ibid., 30.
124. Broderick, ed., *Catholic Encyclopedia*, II.
125. Ibid., 124, 65, 99, 151, 218, 225, 291, 401-403, 467, 523, 528, 583.
126. E.g., Carson, *Dawn or Twilight?* 37.
127. Cf. Kung, *Infallible?* 68.
128. Broderick, ed., *Catholic Encyclopedia*, 1, 581.
129. Ibid., 366, emphasis added.
130. Carson, *Dawn or Twilight?* 46.
131. Schrotenboer, ed., *Roman Catholicism: A Contemporary Evangelical Perspective*, 47.
132. Broderick, ed., *Catholic Encyclopedia*, 203.
133. Ibid., 292, 596.
134. Ibid., 434.
135. August Bernard Hasler, *How the Pope Became Infallible: Pius IX and the Politics of Persuasion* (Garden City, NY: Doubleday, 1981), 310; cf. *Papal Power: Its Origins and Development*.
136. Carson, *Dawn or Twilight?* 72.
137. Cf. Wells, *Revolution in Rome*, 132.
138. Pope Paul VI, *Devotion*, 20.
139. E.g., cf. Broderick, ed., *Catholic Encyclopedia*, 374-375.
140. Abbott, ed., *Documents of Vatican II*, 94-95.
141. Broderick, ed., *Catholic Encyclopedia*, 370.
142. Ott, *Fundamentals of Catholic Dogma*, 214, emphasis added.
143. Ibid.
144. R.C. Sproul, "The Virgin Mary," transcribed lecture (1987), 5.
145. Ibid., 6; cf. Ott, *Fundamentals of Catholic Dogma*, 203-213; and Pope Paul VI, *Devotion*, 15.
146. Abbott, ed., *Documents of Vatican II*, 91.
147. Peter M.J. Stravinskas, *The Catholic Response* (Huntington, IN: Our Sunday Visitor, 1985), 80.
148. Ott, *Fundamentals of Catholic Dogma*, 211.
149. Broderick, ed., *Catholic Encyclopedia*, 285.
150. Ott, *Fundamentals of Catholic Dogma*, 213.
151. Carson, *Dawn or Twilight?* 129.
152. See www.vatican.va, Holy See press office.
153. See Ken Raggio, "The Spirit of Mary in the Catholic Church," www.kenraggio.com, June, 21, 2002.
154. "Act of Consecration to Our Lady" *Fatima Crusader* magazine, taken from www.fatima.org.
155. Schrotenboer, ed., *Roman Catholicism: A Contemporary Evangelical Perspective*, 31.
156. E.g., Ott, *Fundamentals of Catholic Dogma*, 200, 208, 214; Keating, *Catholicism and Fundamentalism*, 275, 279.
157. "Evangelicals & Catholics Together: The Christian Mission in the Third Millennium," May 1994, taken from www.leaderu.com, emphasis added.
158. "Graham Continues to Send to Catholicism," *The Flaming Torch* (April/May/June 1998, vol. 39, no 2), 5. Billy Graham's son, Franklin, follows his father's leading regarding Catholicism.
159. Broderick, ed., *Catholic Encyclopedia*, 270.
160. Ibid., 402.
161. Ibid., 585.
162. Ibid., 539.